The Squirrel Family Acorn

Kristin Lehr

ISBN 978-1-64191-976-0 (paperback)
ISBN 978-1-64191-979-1 (hardcover)
ISBN 978-1-64191-977-7 (digital)

Christian Faith Publishing, Inc.
832 Park Avenue
Meadville, PA 16335
www.christianfaithpublishing.com

Printed in the United States of America

To the Christian Mafia, love you forever!

This is the Squirrel family acorn.

Thank you, God; all good things come from you.

This is the sprout that sprung from the Squirrel family acorn.

Thank you, God; all good things come from you.

This is the rain that watered the sprout that sprung from the Squirrel family acorn.

Thank you, God; all good things come from you.

This is the tree that grew from the rain that watered the sprout that sprung from the Squirrel family acorn.

Thank you, God; all good things come from you.

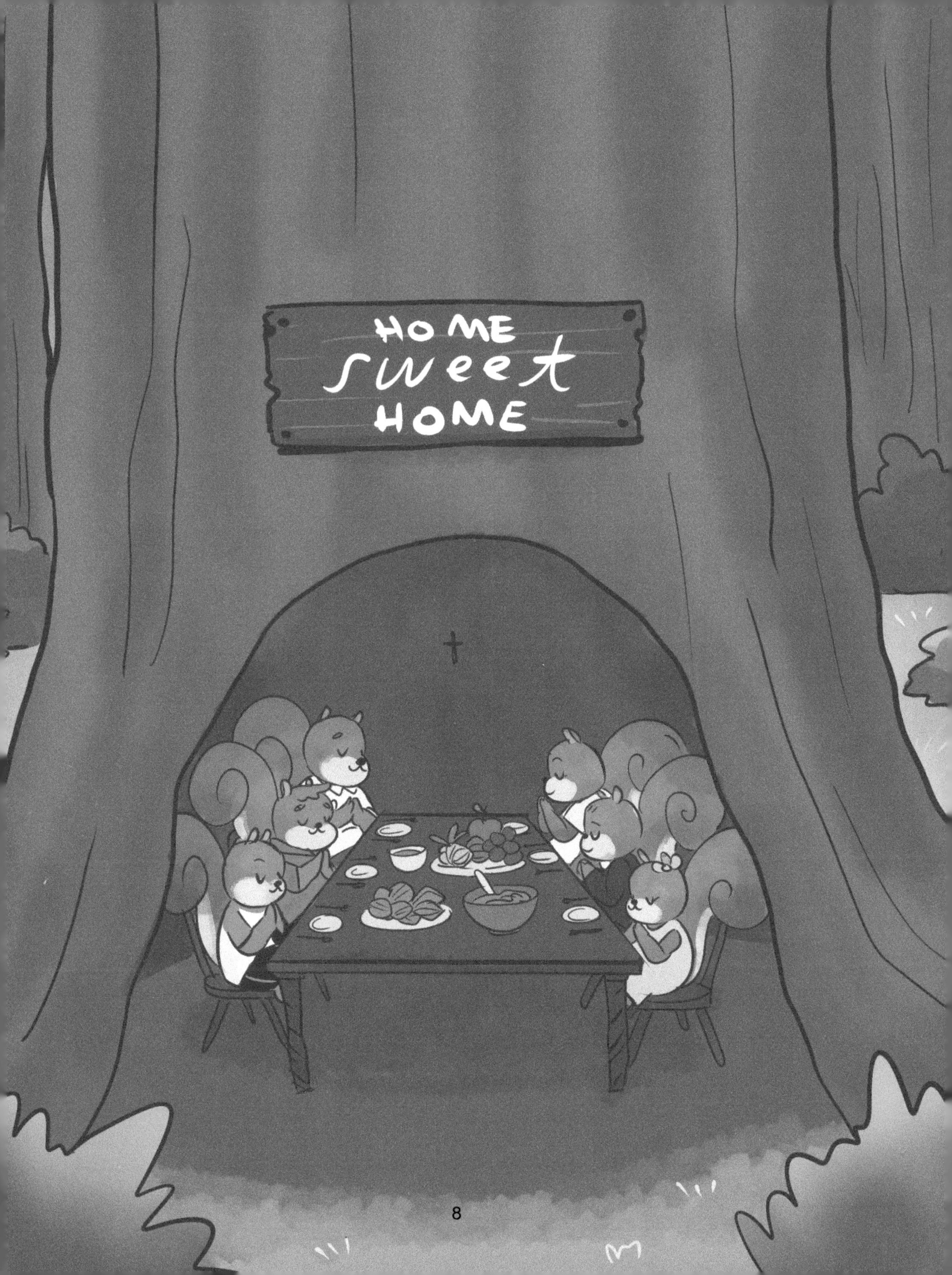
HOME
sweet
HOME

These are the birds who live in the tree that grew from the rain that watered the sprout that sprung from the Squirrel family acorn.

Thank you, God; all good things come from you.

This is the nest built by the birds who live in the tree that grew from the rain that watered the sprout that sprung from the Squirrel family acorn.

Thank you, God; all good things come from you.

These are the eggs that rest in the nest built by the birds who live in the tree that grew from the rain that watered the sprout that sprung from the Squirrel family acorn.

Thank you, God; all good things come from you.

These are the chicks who *pop* from the eggs that rest in the nest built by the birds who live in the tree that grew from the rain that watered the sprout that sprung from the Squirrel family acorn.

Thank you, God; all good things come from you.

"Peep, peep, peep," chirp the chicks who *pop* from the eggs that rest in the nest built by the birds who live in the tree that grew from the rain that watered the sprout that sprung from the Squirrel family acorn.

Thank you, God; all good things come from you.

This is the mama hearing the peeps chirped by the chicks who *pop* from the eggs that rest in the nest built by the birds who live in the tree that grew from the rain that watered the sprout that sprung from the Squirrel family acorn.

Thank you, God; all good things come from you.

These are the worms brought by the mama hearing the peeps chirped by the chicks who *pop* from the eggs that rest in the nest built by the birds who live in the tree that grew from the rain that watered the sprout that sprung from the Squirrel family acorn.

Thank you, God; all good things come from you.

This is the storm that called the worms brought by the mama who hears the peeps chirped by the chicks who *pop* from the eggs that rest in the nest built by the birds who live in the tree that grew from the rain that watered the sprout that sprung from the Squirrel family acorn.

Thank you, God; all good things come from you.

This is the sun shining after the storm that called the worms brought by the mama who hears the peeps chirped by the chicks who *pop* from the eggs that rest in the nest built by the birds who live in the tree that grew from the rain that watered the sprout that sprung from the Squirrel family acorn.

Thank you, God; all good things come from you.

This is the rainbow that paints the sky behind the sun shining after the storm that called the worms brought by the mama who hears the peeps chirped by the chicks who *pop* from the eggs that rest in the nest built by the birds who live in the tree that grew from the rain that watered the sprout that sprung from the Squirrel family acorn.

Thank you, God; all good things come from you.

This is God's promise shown in the rainbow that paints the sky behind the sun shining after the storm that called the worms brought by the mama who hears the peeps chirped by the chicks who *pop* from the eggs that rest in the nest built by the birds who live in the tree that grew from the rain that watered the sprout that sprung from the Squirrel family acorn.

Thank you, God; all good things come from you.

"I love you, my child, and I'm here for you always," is the promise of God shown in the rainbow that paints the sky behind the sun shining after the storm that called the worms brought by the mama who hears the peeps chirped by the chicks who *pop* from the eggs that rest in the nest built by the birds who live in the tree that grew from the rain that watered the sprout that sprung from the Squirrel family acorn.

Thank you, God; all good things come from you.
Scripture Inspiration: James 1:17

About the Author

Dr. Kristin Lehr is the Director of Children's Ministry at Zionsville Presbyterian Church where she has been on staff for a decade. Prior to her work in ministry, Kristin taught fifth grade in Carmel, Indiana, where she continues to reside with her husband, Chip, and three sons, Connor, Carter, and Cooper. In her spare time, Kristin can be found reading or playing tennis or spending time with her besties. Kristin has degrees in Elementary Education, Special Education, Effective Teaching and a PhD in Christian Communication and Leadership. This is her first book, and she attributes the inspiration to the children she teaches and the Great Banquet community.

Follow Kristin on social media @thekristinlehr or kristinlehr.com

CPSIA information can be obtained
at www.ICGtesting.com
Printed in the USA
BVHW020540081019
560431BV00008B/455/P